THE SEVENTH DAY SABBATH,

A PERPETUAL SIGN, FROM THE BEGINNING TO THE ENTERING INTO THE GATES OF THE HOLY CITY, ACCORDING TO THE COMMANDMENT

BY JOSEPH BATES

"Brethren, I write no new commandment unto you, but an old commandment which ye had from the *beginning*. The old commandment is the WORD which ye have heard from the *beginning*." *John* ii: 7.

"In the *beginning* God created the heaven and the earth." Gen. i: 1. "And God blessed the seventh day, and rested from all his work." ii: 3.

"Blessed are they that do his commandments, that they may have right to the tree of life and enter in," &c. *Rev.* xxii: 14.

NEW-BEDFORD
PRESS OF BENJAMIN LINDSEY
1846.

[Pg 1]

PREFACE.
TO THE LITTLE FLOCK.

"Remember the Sabbath day to keep it holy." "Six days work may be done, but the *seventh* is the Sabbath of the Lord thy God: in it thou shalt not do any work." This commandment I conceive to be as binding now as it ever was, and will be to the entering into the "gates of the city." Rev. xxii: 14.

I understand that the *seventh* day Sabbath is not the *least* one, among the ALL things that are to be restored before the second advent of Jesus Christ, seeing that the Imperial and Papal power of Rome, since the days of the Apostles, have changed the seventh day Sabbath to the first day of the week!

Twenty days before God re-enacted and wrote the commandments with his finger on tables of stone, he required his people to keep the Sabbath. Exo. xvi: 27, 30. Here he calls the Sabbath "*my commandments and my laws*." Now the SAVIOR has given his comments on the commandments. See Matt. xxii: 35, 40. "On these two (precepts) hang ALL the law and the prophets." Then it would be impossible for the Sabbath to be left out. A question was asked, what shall I do to inherit eternal life? Says Jesus, "If thou wilt enter into life keep the commandments"—xix. Here he quotes five from the tables of stone. If he did not mean all the rest, then he deceived the lawyer in the two first precepts, love to God and love to man. See also Matt. v: 17, 19, 21, 27, 33. PAUL comments thus. "The law is holy, and the commandments holy, just and good." "Circumcision and uncircumcision is nothing but the keeping the commandments of God." "All the law is fulfilled in one word: thou shalt love thy neighbor as thyself." JOHN says, "the old commandment is the WORD from the beginning."—2, 7. Gen. ii: 3. "He carries us from thence into the gates of the city." Rev. xxii: 14. Here he has particular reference to the Sabbath. JAMES calls it the *perfect*, royal law of liberty, which we are to be doers of, and be judged by. Take out the fourth commandment and the law is imperfect, and we shall fail in one point.

The uncompromising advocate for present truth, which feeds and nourishes the little flock in whatever country or place, is the restorer of all things; one man like John the Baptist, cannot discharge this duty to every kindred, nation, tongue and people, and still remain in one place. The truth is what we want.

Fairhaven, August 1846. JOSEPH BATES.

[Pg 3]

THE SABBATH.
FIRST QUESTION IS, WHEN WAS THE SABBATH INSTITUTED?

Those who are in the habit of reading the Scriptures just as they find them, and of understanding them according to the established rules of interpretation, will never be at a loss to understand so plain a passage as the following: "And God blessed the seventh day, and sanctified it; because that in it he had rested from all his work which God created and made." Gen. ii: 3. Moses, when referring to it, says to the children of Israel, "This is that which the Lord hath *said*, to-morrow is the REST of *the* holy Sabbath unto the Lord." Exod. xvi: 23.

Then we understand that God established the seventh day Sabbath in Paradise, on the very day when he rested from all his work, and not one week, nor one year, nor two thousand five hundred and fourteen years afterwards, as some would have it. Is it not plain that the Sabbath was instituted to commemorate the stupendous work of creation, and designed by God to be celebrated by his worshipers as a weekly Sabbath, in the same manner as the Israelites were commanded to celebrate the Passover, from the very night of their deliverance till the resurrection of Jesus from the dead; or as we, as a nation, annually celebrate our national independence; or as type answers to antetype, so we believe this must run down, to the "keeping of the Sabbath to the people of God" in the immortal state.

It is argued by some, that because no mention is made of the Sabbath from its institution in Paradise till the falling of the manna in the wilderness, mentioned in Exo. xvi: 15, that it was therefore *here* instituted for the Jews, but [Pg 4]we think there is bible argument sufficient to sustain the reply of Jesus to the Pharisees, "that the Sabbath was made for MAN and not man for the Sabbath." If it was made for any one exclusively it must have been for Adam, the father of us all, two thousand years before Abraham (who is claimed as the father of the Jews) was born. John says, the old commandment was from the beginning—1: ii: 7.

There is pretty strong inference that the antideluvians measured time by weeks from the account given by Noah, when the waters of the deluge began to subside. He "sent out a dove which soon returned." At the end of *seven* days he sent her out again; and at the end of *seven* days more, he sent her out a third time. Now why this preference for the number *seven*? why not five or ten days, or any other number? Can it be supposed that his fixing on upon *seven* was accidental? How much more natural to conclude that it was in obedience to the authority of God, as expressed in the 2d chap. of Gen. A similar division of time is incidentally mentioned in Gen. xxix:—"fulfill her *week* and we will give thee this also; and Jacob did so and fulfilled her *week*." Now the word *week* is every where used in Scripture as we use it; it never means more nor less than *seven* days (except as symbols of years) and one of them was in all other cases the Sabbath. But now suppose there had been an entire silence on the subject of the Sabbath for this twenty-five hundred years, would that be sufficient evidence that there was none. If so, we have the same evidence that there was no Sabbath from the reign of Joshua till the reign of David, four hundred and six years, as no mention is made of it in the history of that period. But who can be persuaded that Samuel and the pious Judges of Israel did not regard the Sabbath. What does God say of Abraham? that he "obeyed my voice, and kept my charge, my *commandments*, my *statutes* and my *laws*." (See what he calls them in Exo. xvi: 27, 30.) This, of course, includes the whole. Then Abraham reverenced God's Sabbath. Once more, there is no mention of the circumcision from the days of Joshua till the days of Jeremiah, a period of more than eight hundred years. Will it be believed that Samuel and David, and all those pious worthies with the whole Jewish nation, neglected that essential seal of the covenant for eight hundred years? It cannot be admitted for a moment. How [Pg 5]then can any one suppose from the alleged silence of the sacred history that Adam, Enoch, Noah and Abraham, kept no Sabbath, because the fact was not stated? If we turn to Jer. ix: 25, 26, we find that they had not neglected this right of circumcision, only they had not circumcised their hearts; so that the proof is clear, that silence respecting the keeping any positive command of God, is no evidence that it is not in full force.

Again, if the Sabbath was not instituted in Paradise, why did Moses mention it in connection with the creation of the world? Why not reserve this fact for two or three thousand years in his history, until the manna fell in the wilderness, (see Exo. xvi: 23) and then state that the seventh day Sabbath commenced, as *some* will have it? I answer, for the very best of reasons, that it did not commence there. Let us examine the text. "And it came to pass, that on the sixth day they gathered twice as much bread as on any preceding day, and *all the rulers of the congregation came and told Moses*. And he said unto them this is that which the Lord hath said, *to-morrow is the rest of the holy Sabbath*, bake that which ye will bake, &c. &c." If this had been the establishing of the holy Sabbath and Moses had said to-morrow *shall be* the Sabbath, then would it have been clear; but no, he speaks as familiarly about it as we do when we say that to-morrow is the Sabbath, showing conclusively that it was known before, or how could the people have known that they must gather two day's manna on Friday the sixth day, unless they had had some previous knowledge of the Sabbath? for Moses had already taught them not to "leave any of it until the morning"—v. 19. The 20th verse shows that the Sabbath had not yet come since their receiving the manna, because it spoiled and "bred worms by the next morning;" whereas, on the Sabbath morning it was found sweet and eatible—24th v. This was the thirtieth day after leaving Egypt (1st v.) and twenty days before it was given on Sinai. The weekly Sabbath then was appointed before this or before the days of Moses. Where was it then? Answer, in the second chapter of Genesis and no where else; and the same week on which the manna fell, the weekly Sabbath was revived among or with God's chosen people. Grotius tells us "that the memory of the creation's being performed in seven days, was preserved not only among the Greeks and Italians, but among the Celts and Indians." Other [Pg 6]writers say Assyrians, Egyptians, Arabians, Britons and Germans, all of whom divide their time into weeks. Philo says "the Sabbath is not peculiar to any one people or country, but is common to all the world." Josephus states "that there is no city either of Greeks or barbarians or any *other nation*, where the religion of the Sabbath is not known." But as they, like the great mass of God's professed people in christendom, paid little or no heed to what God had said about the particular day, (except the Jews, and a few others) they (as we are informed in history) adopted peculiar days to suit themselves, viz: the christian nations chose to obey the Pope of Rome, who changed the *seventh* day Sabbath to the first day, and call it the holy Sabbath; the Persians selected Monday; the Grecians Tuesday; the Assyrians Wednesday; the Egyptians Thursday; the Turks Friday, and the Jews the seventh day, Saturday, as God had commanded. Three standing miracles a week, for about forty years annually, ought to perpetuate the Sabbath. 1st, double the quantity of manna on the sixth day; 2d, none on the seventh; 3d, did not spoil on the seventh day. If it does not matter which day you keep holy to the Lord, then all these nations are right. Now reflect one moment on this, and then open your bible and read the commandment of the God of all these nations! "REMEMBER! (what you have been taught before) *the Sabbath day to keep it holy*," (which day is it Lord?) "*the* SEVENTH *is the Sabbath of the Lord thy God: in it thou shalt not do any work, thou nor thy son, nor thy daughter, thy man servant nor thy maid servant, nor thy cattle, nor thy stranger, that is within thy gates.*" Who is the stranger? (Gentiles.) Now the reason for it will carry us back again to Paradise. "*For in six days the Lord made heaven and earth, the sea, and all that in them is, and rested on the* SEVENTH; *wherefore the Lord blessed the Sabbath day and hallowed it.*" "Wherefore the children of Israel shall keep the Sabbath, to observe the *Sabbath* throughout their generations for a *perpetual covenant*; it is a SIGN between me and the children of Israel *forever.*" (Why is it Lord?) "*For in six days the Lord made heaven and earth, and on the* SEVENTH *day he rested and was refreshed.*" Exo. xx and xxxi. Which day now will you choose? O, says the reader, the seventh if I knew which of the days it was. If you don't know, why are you so sure that the *first* day is right? O,[Pg 7]because the history of the world has settled that, and this is the most we can know. Very well then, does not the *seventh* come the day before the eighth? If we have not got the days of the week right now, it is not likely that we ever shall. God does not require of us any more than what we know; by that we shall be judged. Luke xxiii: 55, 56.

Once more: think you that the spirit of God ever directed Moses when he was giving the history of the creation of the world, to write that he (God) "blessed the *seventh* day and sanctified it, because that in it he had rested from all his work," unless he meant it to be dated from that very day? Why, this is as clear to the unbiassed mind as it is that God created man the sixth day. Would it not be the height of absurdity to attempt to prove that God only intended Adam should be created at some future period, or that the creation of the heavens and earth was not in the beginning, but some twenty-five hundred years afterward? All this would be as cogent reasoning as it would be to argue that God did not intend this day of *rest* should commence until about twenty-five hundred years afterwards. (The word Sabbath signifies rest.)

It follows then irresistibly, that the weekly Sabbath was not made for the Jews only, (but as Jesus says, for 'man') for the Jews had no existence until more than two thousand years after it was established. President Humphrey in his essays on the Sabbath says, "That he (God) instituted it when he rested from all his work, on the *seventh* day of the first week, and gave it primarily to our first parents, and through them to all their posterity; that the observance of it was enjoined upon the children of Israel soon after they left Egypt, not in the form of a new enactment, but as an ancient institution which was far from being forgotten, though it had doubtless been greatly neglected under the cruel domination of their heathen masters; that it was reenacted with great pomp and solemnity, and written in stone by the finger of God at Sinai; that the sacred institution then took the form of a statute, with explicit prohibitions and requirements, and has never been repealed or altered since; that it can never expire of itself, because it has no limitation."

In Deut. vii: 6-8, God gives his reasons for selecting the Jews to keep his covenant in preference to any other nation; only seventy at first—x: 22. God calls it his [Pg 8]"Sabbath," and refers us right back to the creation for proof. "For in six days the Lord made heaven and earth and sea, and all that in them is, and rested on the *seventh*," &c. Here then we stand fixed by the immutable law of God, and the word of Jesus, that "the Sabbath was made for man!" Paul says, "there is no respect of persons with God." Rom. ii: 11. Isaiah shows us plainly that the Jew is not the only one to be blessed for keeping the Sabbath. He says "Blessed is the *man* (are not the Gentiles men) that keepeth the Sabbath from polluting it." "Also the sons of the stranger, (who are these if they are not Gentiles?) every one that keepeth the Sabbath from polluting it, (does he mean me? yes, every Gentile in the universe, or else he respects persons) even them will I bring to my holy mountain and make them joyful in my house of prayer; for my house shall be called an house of prayer for *all* people." Isa. lvi: 2, 6, 7. If this promise is not to the Gentile as well as the Jew, then "*the* house of prayer for all people" is no promise to the Gentile.

Now we ask, if God has ever abrogated the law of the Sabbath? If he has it can easily be found. We undertake to say without fear of contradiction, he has not made any such record in the bible; but to the contrary, he calls it a perpetual covenant, a "sign between me and the children of Israel forever," for the reason that he rested on the seventh day. Exo. xxxi: 16, 17. Says one, has not the ceremonial law been annulled and nailed to the cross? Yes, but what of that? Why then the Sabbath must be abolished, for Paul says so! Where? Why in Cols. 2d chapter, and xiv. Romans. How can you think that God ever inspired Paul to say that the *seventh* day Sabbath was made void or nailed to the cross at the crucifixion, when he never intended any such change; if he did, he certainly would have deceived the inhabitants of Jerusalem, in the promise which he made them about two thousand four hundred and forty-six years ago! Turn now to Jer. xvii: 25, and tell me if he did not promise the inhabitants of Jerusalem that their city should remain forever if they would hallow the Sabbath day. Now suppose the inhabitants of Jerusalem had entered into this agreement, and entailed it upon their posterity (because you see it could not have been fulfilled unless it had continued from generation to generation,) to keep the Sabbath holy, would not God have been bound to let Jerusalem remain forever? You say [Pg 9]yes. Well, then, I ask you to shew how he could have kept that promise inviolate if he intended in less than six hundred and fifty years to change this seventh day Sabbath, and call the first day of the week the Sabbath, or abolish it altogether? I say, therefore, if there has been any change one way or the other in the Sabbath, since that promise, it would be impossible to understand any other promise in the Bible; how much more reasonable to believe God than man. If men will allow themselves to believe the monstrous absurdity that FOREVER, as in this promise, ended at the resurrection, then they can easily believe that the Sabbath was changed from the *seventh* to the first day of the week. Or if they choose the other extreme, abolished until the people of God should awake to be clothed on with immortality. Heb. iv: 9.

Now does it not appear plain that the Sabbath is from God, and that it is coeval and co-extensive (as is the institution of marriage) with the world. That it is without limitation; that there is not one thus saith the Lord that it ever was or ever will be abolished, in time or eternity.—See Exod. xxxi: 16, 17; and Isa. lxvi: 22, 24; Heb. iv: 4, 9. But let us return and look at the subject as we have commenced in the light of Paul's argument to the Romans and Collossians, for here is where all writers on this subject, for the change or the overthrow of the *seventh* day Sabbath attempt to draw their strong arguments. The second question then, is this:

HAS THE SABBATH BEEN ABOLISHED SINCE THE SEVENTH DAY OF CREATION?
IF SO, WHEN, AND WHERE IS THE PROOF?

The text already referred to, is in Rom. xiv: 5, 6.—"One man esteemeth one day above another; another esteemeth every day alike. Let every man be persuaded in his own mind. He that regardeth the day, regardeth it unto the Lord; and he that regardeth not the day to the Lord, he doth not regard it." Does the apostle here mean to say, that under the new or Christian dispensation it is a matter of indifference which day of the week is kept as a Sabbath, or whether any Sabbath at all is kept? Was that institution which the people of God had been commanded to call a delight, the holy of the Lord, honorable, now to be esteemed of so carnal a nature as to be ranked among [Pg 10]the things which Jesus "took out of the way, nailing it to his cross." If this be true, then has Jesus, in the same manner, abolished the eight last verses in the fifty-eighth of Isaiah, and the 2d, 6th and 7th verses of the 56th chapter have no reference to the Gentile since the crucifixion. O Lord help us rightly to understand and divide thy word. But is it not evident from the four first verses in the same chapter of Romans, that Paul is speaking of feast days; giving them again in substance the decrees which had been given by the Apostles in their first conference, in A. D. 51, held at Jerusalem. See Acts xv: 19. James proposes their letter to the Gentiles should be "that they abstain from pollution of Idols, and from fornication, and from things strangled, and from blood;" to which the conference all agreed. Now please read their unanimous *decrees* (xvi: 4,) from twenty-three to thirty verses. "For it seemed good to the Holy Ghost and to us, to lay upon you no greater burden than these necessary things." "That ye abstain from meats offered to Idols, and from blood, and from things strangled, and from fornication, from which if ye keep yourselves ye shall do well." Reading along to the 13th of the next chapter, we find Paul establishing the Churches with these decrees; (see 4, 5,) and at Philippi he holds his meeting, (not in the Jews Synagogue) but at the river's side, on the *Sabbath* day. A little from this it is said that Paul is in Thesalonica preaching on the Sabbath days. Luke says this was his*manner*! What was it? Why, to preach on the Sabbath days, (not 1st days.) Observe here was three Sabbaths in succession. xvii: 2. A little while from this Paul locates himself in Corinth, and there preaches to the Jews and Greeks (or Gentiles) a year and six months *every Sabbath*. Now this must have been seventy-eight in succession. xviii: 4, 11. Does this look like abolishing the Sabbath day? Has anything been said about the 1st day yet? No, we shall speak of that by and by.

Before this he was in Antioch. "And when the Jews were gone out of the synagogue the GENTILES besought that these words might be preached to them the next Sabbath. And the next Sabbath day came almost the whole city together to hear the word of God." xiii: 42, 44. Here is proof that the Gentiles kept the Sabbath. Now I wish to place the other strong text which is so strangely adhered to for abolishing or changing this [Pg 11]Sabbath along side of this, that we may understand his meaning. "Blotting out the hand-writing of ordinances that was against us, which was contrary to us, and took it out of the way, nailing it to his cross."

"Let no man therefore judge you in meat, or in drink, or in respect of a holy day, or of the new moon, or of the Sabbath days." Coll. ii: 14, 16. Now here is one of the strong arguments adhered to by all those who say the seventh day Sabbath was abolished at the crucifixion of our Lord; while on the other hand by the great mass of the Christian world, (so called,) the seventh day Sabbath ceased here, and in less than forty-eight hours the change was made to the first day of the week. Now remember Paul's manner, (before stated) itinerating from city to city and nation to nation, always preaching to Jews and Gentiles on the seventh day Sabbath, (for there is no other day called the Lord's Sabbath in the Bible.) Now if the Apostle did mean to include the Sabbath of the Lord God with the Jewish feasts and Sabbaths in the text, then the course he took to do so, was the strangest imaginable. His *manner* always was, as recorded, with the exception of one night, to preach on the very day that he was laboring to abolish. If you will look at the date in your bibles, you will learn this same apostle had been laboring in this way as a special messenger to the Gentiles, between twenty and thirty years since (as you say) the Sabbath was changed or abolished, and yet never uttered one word with respect to any other day in the week to be set apart as a holy day or Sabbath. I understand all the arguments about his laboring in the Jewish

Synagogue on their Sabbath, because they were open for worship on that day, &c., but he did not always preach in their Synagogues. He says that he preached the Kingdom of God, and labored in his own hired house for two years. He also established a daily meeting for disputation in the school of Tyranus. Acts xix: 9. Again he says, I have "kept *back* NOTHING that was PROFITABLE *unto you.* (Now if the Sabbath had been changed or abolished, would it not have been *profitable* to have told them so?) and have taught you publicly, and from house to house." "For I have not shunned to declare unto you ALL the council of God."—Acts xx: 20, 27. Then it is clear that he taught them by example that the Sabbath of the Lord God was not abolished. Luke says it was the *custom* (or manner) of Christ [Pg 12]to teach in the synagogues on the Sabbath day. iv: 16, 31. Mark says, "And when the Sabbath day was come he began to teach in their synagogue." Mark vi: 2.—Now if Jesus was about to abolish or change this Sabbath, (which belonged to the first code, the moral law, and not the ceremonial, the second code, which was to be nailed to his cross, or rather, as said the angel Gabriel to Daniel, ix: 27, "he (Christ) in the midst of the week shall cause the *sacrifice* and*oblation* to cease," meaning that the Jewish sacrifices and offerings would cease at his death.) Jesus did not attend to any of the ceremonies of the Jews except the passover and the feasts of tabernacles. Why did he say, "Think not I am come to destroy the *law* or the prophets? I am not come to destroy but fulfill. One jot or one title shall in no wise pass from the *law* 'till all be fulfilled." "Whosoever therefore shall break one of these least commandments" &c. Did he mean the ten commandments? Yes; for he immediately points out the third, not to take God's name in vain; sixth and seventh, not to kill nor to commit adultery, and styles them the *least*. Then the others, which include the fourth, of course were greater than these. Matt. v: 17, 19, 21, 27, 23, and were not to be broken nor pass away. Then the Sabbath stands unchanged.

Almost every writer which I have read on the subject of abolishing or changing the seventh day Sabbath, call it the Jewish Sabbath, hence their difficulty. How can it be the Jewish Sabbath when it was established two thousand years before there was a Jew on the face of the earth, and certainly twenty-five hundred before it was embodied in the decalogue, or re-enacted and written in stone by the finger of God at Sinai. God called this HIS *Sabbath*, and Jesus says it was made for man, (not particularly for the Jews.)

"Well," says one, "what is the meaning of the texts which you have quoted, where it speaks of Sabbaths?"—Answer: These are the Jewish Sabbaths! which belong to them as a nation and are connected with their feasts. God by Hosea makes this distinction, and says, "I will also cause all *her* mirth to cease, her feast days, her new moons and *her* Sabbaths, and all her solemn feasts." These then belong to the text quoted, and not God's Sabbath. Do you ask for the proof? See xxiii Levit. 4. "*These are the* FEASTS *of the Lord, which ye shall proclaim in their* [Pg 13]*seasons,* EVERY THING UPON HIS DAY"—37th v. (May we not deviate a little? If you do it will be at your peril.) Fifteenth and sixteenth verses gives them a fifty day's Sabbath; twenty-fourth verse says: "Speak unto the children of Israel, saying in the seventh month in the first day of the month, shall ye have a *Sabbath*, a memorial of blowing of trumpets, an holy convocation."

"Also on the tenth day of the seventh month there shall be a day of atonement. It shall be unto you a*Sabbath* of rest." 27, 32.

"Also on the fifteenth day of the seventh month when ye shall have gathered in the fruit of the land, ye shall keep a feast unto the Lord seven days. On the first shall be a Sabbath, and on the eighth day shall be a Sabbath. 39v. And Moses *declared* unto the children of Israel the FEASTS of the Lord." 44v. Now here we have FOUR kinds of *Jewish* Sabbaths, also *called* "FEASTS *of the Lord*," to be kept annually. The first fifty days or seven weeks Sabbath ends the third month, seventh. In three months and twenty-four days more commences the second Sabbath, seventh month, first; the next, the tenth; the last the fifteenth of the month. Between the first two Sabbaths there is an interval of one hundred and twelve days; the next two, ten days, and the next, five days. Now it can be seen at a glance, that neither of these Sabbaths could be on the seventh day any oftener than other annual feast could come on that day. These then are what Hosea calls HER Sabbaths. Paul calls them HOLY DAYS, *new moons, and Sabbaths*; and this is what they are stated to be. The first day of the seventh month is a *new moon* SABBATH, the tenth is a Sabbath of rest and

Holy convocation, a day of atonement, and the fifteenth a feast of Sabbaths. Do you ask for any more evidence that these are the Jewish Sabbaths, and that God's Sabbath is separate from them? Read then what God directed Moses to write in the third verse: "Six days shall work be done, but the *seventh* day is the Sabbath of rest, an holy convocation, ye shall do no work therein, it is the Sabbath of the LORD in all your dwellings." Now Moses has here declared from the mouth of the Lord, that these are ALL the feast of the Lord, (there is no more nor less) and every thing is to be upon *his day*, and he has clearly and definitely separated his Sabbath from the other four. And in the 28th and 29th chapters of Numbers the sacrifices [Pg 14]and offerings for each of these days are made so plain, beginning with the Sabbath, 9v, that we have only to read the following to understand. 26. xxix: 1. First day, seventh month, (new moon;) 7v, 10th day Sabbath; 12v; 15th day Sabbath, and 35v, 23d day Sabbath. And in the days of Nehemiah when Ezra had read the law to the people, viii (more than one thousand years after they were promulgated,) they bound themselves under an oath "to walk in God's law which was given *by the hand of Moses*, the servant of God." "And to observe and *do all the commandments* of the Lord, our Lord." x: 29. And that there might be no misunderstanding about the kind of Sabbaths, they say, "If the people bring ware or any victuals on the Sabbath day to sell, that we would not buy it of them on the Sabbath or on the holy day," (31v.) but they would "charge themselves yearly with a third part of a shekel" (to pay for) "the burnt*offerings* of the *Sabbaths*, of the *new moons*, for the *set feasts*," &c. (33v.) for the house of God, including what has already been set forth in Leviticus and Numbers. Now as their feast days commenced and ended with a Sabbath, so when their feasts ceased to be binding on them these Sabbaths must also, and all were "nailed to the cross." Now I ask if there is one particle of proof that the Sabbath of the Lord is included in these Sabbaths and feast days? Who then dare join them together or contradict the Most High God, and call HIS the *Jewish* Sabbath. *Theirs* was nailed to the cross when Jesus died, while the Lord's is an *everlasting* sign a *perpetual covenant.* The Jews, as a nation, broke their covenant. Jesus and his disciples were one week (the last of the seventy) that is seven years, confirming the new covenant for another people, the Gentiles. Now I ask if this changing the subjects from Jew to Gentile made void the commandments and law of God, or in other words, abolished the fourth commandment; if so, the other nine are not binding. It cannot be that God ever intended to mislead his subjects. Let us illustrate this. Suppose that the Congress of these United States in their present emergency, should promulgate two separate codes of laws, one to be perpetual, the other temporary, to be abolished when peace was proclaimed between this country and Mexico. The time *comes*, the temporary laws are abolished; but strange to hear, a large portion of the people are now insisting upon it that because peace is proclaimed that both [Pg 15]these codes of laws are forever abolished; while another class are *strenuously* insisting that it is only the *fourth* law in the perpetual code that's now abolished, with the temporary and all the rest is still binding. Opposed to all these is a third class, headed by the ministers and scribes of the nation, who are writing and preaching from Maine to Florida, insisting upon it without fear of contradiction, that when peace was proclaimed this fourth law in the perpetual code was to change its date to another day; gradually, (while some of them say immediately) and thenceforward become perpetual, and the other code abolished; and yet not one of these are able to show from the proceedings of Congress that the least alteration had ever been made in the perpetual code. Thus, to me, the case stands clear that neither of the laws or ten commandments in the first code, ever has or ever can be annulled or changed while mortality is stamped on man, for the very reason that God's moral law has no limitation. Jesus then brought in a new covenant, which continued the Sabbath by writing his law upon their hearts. Paul says "written not with ink, but with the spirit of the living God; not in tables of stone, but in fleshy tables of the heart." 2 Cor. iii: 3. And when writing to the Romans he shews *how* the Gentiles are a law unto themselves. He says, they "shew the work of the law written in their hearts, their consciences always bearing them witness, and their thoughts the mean while accusing or else excusing one another," (when will this be Paul) "in the day when God shall judge the secrets of men by Jesus Christ according to my gospel." ii: 15, 16. How plain that this is all the change. The Jews by nature had the law given them on tables of stone, while the Gentiles had the law of commandments written on their hearts. Paul tells the Ephesians that it was "the law of commandments contained in ordinances," (ii: 15) not on tables that were nailed to the cross. If the ten commandments, first written by the finger of God on stone, and then at the second covenant on fleshy tables of the heart, are shadows, can any one tell where we shall find the substance? We are answered, in Christ. Well, hear Isaiah. He says, "that he (Christ) will magnify the law and make it honorable." lxii: 21. Again, I ask, where was the necessity and of what use were the ten commandments written on our hearts, if it was not to render perfect obedience to them. If we do not keep the day God has sanctified, then [Pg 16]we break not the least, but one of the greatest of his commandments. Still, there are many other texts relating to the law, presented by the opposite view, to show that the law respecting the Sabbath is abolished. Let us look at some of them. But it will be necessary in the first place, to make a clear distinction between what is commonly called the

MORAL AND CEREMONIAL LAW.

Bro. S. S. Snow, in writing on this subject about one year ago, in the Jubilee Standard, asks "by what authority this distinction is made." He says "neither our Lord or his apostles made any such distinction. When speaking of the law they never used the terms moral or ceremonial, but always spake of it as a *whole*, calling it *the* law," and further says, "we must have a thus saith the Lord to satisfy us." So I say! I have no doubt but thousands have stopped here; indeed, it has been to me the most difficult point to settle in this whole question. Now let us come to it fairly, and we shall see that the old and new testament writers have ever kept up the distinction, although it may in some parts seem to be one code of laws.

From the twentieth chapter of Exodus, where the law of the Sabbath was re-enacted, and onward, we find two distinct codes of laws. The first was written on two tables of stone with the *finger* of God; the *second* was taken down from his mouth and recorded by the hand of Moses in a book. Paul calls the latter carnal commandments and ordinances, (rites or *ceremonies*) which come under two heads, religious and political, and are Moses's. The first code is God's. For proof see Exo. xvi: 28, 30. "How long refuse ye to keep *my* commandments and *my* laws: see for that the Lord hath given you the Sabbath; and so the people rested on the Sabbath day." Also in the book of Leviticus, where the law of ceremonies is given to the levites or priests, Moses closes with these words: "*These* are the commandments which the Lord commanded Moses for the children of Israel in Mount Sinai;" in Heb. vii: 16, 18, called carnal commandments.

Again, "the Lord said unto Moses, come up to me into the Mount, and be there: and I will give thee tables of stone, and a law, and commandments which I have written." Exo. xxiv: 12. Further he calls them the ten [Pg 17]commandments—xxxiv: 28. And Moses puts them "into the ark"—xl: 20. *Now for the second code of laws.* See Deut. xxxi: 9, 10; and xxiv: 26. "And when Moses had finished writing the law, he commanded them to put *this book* of the LAW (of ceremonies) in the side of the ark of the covenant, to be read at the end of every seven years." This is not the song of deliverance by Moses in the forty-fourth verse of the thirty-second chapter. For, eight hundred and sixty-seven years after this, in the reign of Josiah, king of Israel, the high priest found this book in "the Temple," (2 Chron. xxxiv: 14, 15) which moved all Israel. One hundred and seventy-nine years further onward, Ezra was from morning till noon reading out of this book. Neh. viii: 3; Heb. ix: 19. Paul's comments.

Bro. Snow says in regard to the commandments, "The principles of moral conduct embraced in the law, was binding before the law was given, (meaning that one of course at Mt. Sinai) and is binding *now*; it is immutable and eternal! It is comprehended in one word, LOVE." If he meant, as we believe he did, to comprehend what Jesus did in the xix. and xxii. chap. Matt. 37-40, and Paul, and James, and John after him, then we ask how it is possible for him to reject from that code of laws, the only one, *the seventh day rest*, that was promulgated at the *beginning*, while at the same time the other nine, that were not written until about three thousand years afterwards, were eternally binding; without doubt, the whole ten commandments are co-eval and co-extensive with sin. Again, he says, "We readily admit, that if what is called the decalogue or ten commandments be binding on us, *we ought* to observe the seventh day, for that was appointed by the Lord as the Sabbath day." Let us see if Jesus and his apostles do not make it binding.*First then, the distinction of the two codes by Jesus.*

The Pharisees ask the Saviour why his disciples transgress the tradition of the elders? His answer is, "Why do ye transgress the commandment of God?" and he immediately cites them to the fifth commandment, Matt. xv: 25. Again, "The law and the prophets were until John; since that time the kingdom of God is preached," &c. Luke xvi: 16. Jesus was three years after this introducing the gospel of the kingdom, unwaveringly holding his meetings on the Sabbath days, (which our opponents say were now about to be*abolished*; others say changed,) and never uttering a syllable to show to the contrary, but that this was [Pg 18]and always would be the holy day for worship. Mark says when the Sabbath (the Seventh day, for there was no other,) was come, he began to teach in the Synagogue, vi: 2. Luke says, "as his *custom* was, he went into the Synagogue and taught on the Sabbath day." iv: 16, 31. Will it be said of him as it is of Paul on like occasions, some thirty years afterwards, that he uniformly held his meetings on the Sabbath because he had no where else to preach, or that this day was the only one in the week in which the people would come out to hear him? Every bible reader knows better; witness the five thousand and the seven thousand, and the multitudes that thronged him in the streets, in the cities and towns where they listened to him; besides, he was now establishing a new dispensation, while theirs was passing away. Then he did not follow any of their customs or rites or ceremonies which he had come to abolish.

I have already quoted Matt. v: 17, 18, where Jesus said he had come to fulfil the law, and immediately begins by showing them that they are not to violate one of the least of the commandments, and cites them to some—see vi: 19, 21, 27, 33. Again, he is tauntingly asked "which is the great commandment in the law: Jesus said unto him, thou shalt love the Lord thy God with all thy heart, and with all thy soul, and with all thy mind. This is the *first* and great commandment. And the second is like unto it, Thou shalt love thy neighbor as thyself. On these two commandments hang all the law and the prophets." xxii: 36, 40. Here Jesus has divided the ten commandments into two parts, or as it is written on two tables of stone. The first four on the first table treat of those duties which we owe to God—the other six refers to those which we owe to man, requiring perfect obedience.

Once more, "One came and said unto him, good master what good thing shall I do that I may have eternal life? He said, If thou wilt enter into life keep the commandments. Then he asked him which? He cited him to the last part of what he called the second, loving his neighbor as himself." If he had cited him to the first table, as in the xxii, quoted above, he could not have replied "*all* these have I kept from my youth up." Why? Because he would have already been perfect, for Jesus in reply to his question, what he should do to inherit eternal life, said he must "keep the commandments." Matt. xix: 16-20. Is not the Sabbath included in these commandments? Surely [Pg 19]it is! Then how absurd to believe that Jesus, just at the close of his ministry, should teach that the way, the only way, to enter into life, was to keep the commandments, one of which was to be abolished in a few months from that time, without the least intimation from him or his Father that it was to take place. I say again, if the Sabbath is abolished, we ask those who teach it to cite us to the chapter and verse, not to the law of rites and ceremonies which are abolished, for we have already shown that the Sabbath was instituted more than twenty-five hundred years before Moses wrote the carnal ordinances or ceremonies. God said, "Abraham kept *my* charge, *my* commandments, *my*statutes, and *my* laws." Gen. xxvi: 5. This must include the Sabbath, for the Sabbath was the first law given, therefore if Abraham did not keep the Sabbath, I cannot understand what commandments, statutes and laws mean in this chapter. Jesus says, "As I have kept my Father's commandments," John xv: 10. Did he keep the commandments? Yes. Mark and Luke, before quoted—(but more of this in another place.)

In John vii: 19, Jesus speaks of "Moses law," "*your law*." x: 34. Again, "*their law*." xv: 25. Here then we show that Jesus kept up a clear distinction between what God calls *my* law and commandments and Moses law, "*their* law," "*your* law." Let us now look at the argument of the Apostles. Paul preaching at Antioc taught the Brethren that by Jesus Christ all who believed in him "are justified from all things, from which ye could not be justified by the *Law of Moses.*" Acts xiii: 39.

The Pharisees said "that it was needful to circumcise them and commend them to keep the *Law of Moses.*" xv: 5.

Again, when Paul had come to Jerusalem the second time, (fourteen years from the time he met the Apostles in conference where they established the decrees for the churches. See Acts xx: 19; Gal. ii: 1,) the Apostles shewed him how many thousands of Jews there were which believed and were zealous of the *law*: "And they are informed of thee, that thou teachest *all* the Jews which are among the Gentiles to forsake *Moses* and the *customs*." xxi: 20, 21. Any person who will carefully read the eight chapters here included, must be thoroughly convinced that the Apostle's troubles were about the law of ceremonies written and given by Moses, and nothing to do with the ten commandments. For you see a little before he comes to Jerusalem, he had been preaching at Corinth every [Pg 20]Sabbath for eighteen months. xxiii: 4, 11. And this, be it remembered, was more than twenty years after the Jewish Sabbaths and ceremonies were nailed to the cross.—And you see that Paul was the man above all the Apostles to be persecuted on account of the abolition of the Jews' law of ceremonies, for he was the "*great* Apostle to the Gentiles:" and if the "Sabbath of the Lord our God" was to have been abolished when the Saviour died, Paul was the very man selected for that purpose. It is clear, therefore, that he did not abolish the seventh day Sabbath among the Gentiles. This same Apostle tells the Romans "that Christ is the end of the law for righteousness to every one that believeth." x: 4. Again, that "sin shall not have dominion over you, for ye are not under the *law* but under grace." vi: 14. Once more: He says the Gentiles having not the *law*, are a*law* unto themselves. Why? Because, he says in the next verse, it shows the *law* written on their hearts. The law of ceremonies? No; that which was on tables of stone. ii: 14-16. We might quote much more which looks like embracing the whole law. Let us now look at a few texts in the same letter, which will draw a distinguishing line between the two codes of laws. Paul, in the vii ch. 9-13v. brings to view the carnal commandment, and the one unto life, and sums up his argument in these words: "Wherefore the *law* is holy, and the commandment holy and just and good." In the 7v he quotes from the decalogue. Again, he that loveth another hath fulfilled the *law*. How? Why thou shalt not steal, nor commit adultery, nor bear false witness, nor covet, thou shalt love thy neighbor as thyself. Therefore *love* is the fulfilling of the law. Rom. xiii: 8, 10.—This then is what the Saviour taught the young man to do to secure "eternal life." Matt. Once more, in concluding a long argument on the law in Rom. iii: 31, he closes with this language: "Do we then make void the law through faith? God forbid ye, *we establish* the *law*."—What *law* is here established? not the law of rites and ceremonies. What then, for Paul means some *law*. It can be no other than what he calls the law of "life," of "love," the ten commandments. How could even that be established twenty-nine years after the crucifixion, if one of the *greatest* commandments had been abolished out of the code, that is the Sabbath.

Paul's letter to the Corinthians teaches that "circumcision is nothing, and uncircumcision is nothing but the *keeping* [Pg 21]of the commandments of God." vii: 19. Again, in his epistle to the Galatians, his phraseology is somewhat changed, but the argument is to the same point, although some passages read as though every vestage of *law* was swept by the board when Jesus hung upon the cross. For instance, such as the following: "But that no man is justified by the *law* in the sight of God it is evident, for the just shall live by faith, and the LAW is not of faith, but the man that doeth them shall live by them." "Christ hath redeemed us from the curse of the *law*, being made a curse for us." "But before faith came we were kept under the *law*, shut up unto the faith which should afterwards be revealed." "Wherefore the law was our schoolmaster to bring us unto Christ that we might be justified by faith, but after that faith has come we are no longer under a schoolmaster." Gal. iii: 11-13, 23-25. Again: "For as many as are of the works of the *law* are under the curse." 10v. Now are we to understand from these texts that whosoever continueth in the *law* is cursed, and that the law, *the whole law*, was abolished when Christ came as our schoolmaster, he being the "end of the law?" Rom. x: 4. If so, how is it possible for any man, even Paul himself, to be saved. But we do not believe that Paul taught these brethren any different doctrine than what has already been shown in the Acts, Romans, and Corinthians, and also the Eph., Phil., Col., and Heb. If he did not mean the law written by the hand of Moses, distinguishing it from the *law* of the ten commandments, written by the finger of God on tables of stone, then pray tell me if you can, what he means (in the closing of this argument,) by saying, "For *all* the LAW is FULFILLED in one word, even this: Thou shalt love thy neighbor as thyself." v: 14. Surely he is quoting the Saviour's words in Matt. xxii: 39, relative to the commandment of the Lord our God. To his son Timothy he says: "Now the end of the commandment is charity," (love) meaning of course the *last* part of the ten commandments. In vi: 2, he says: "Bear ye one anothers burdens and so fulfil the *law* of Christ." Does this differ from the *law* God? Yes, a little, for it is the new commandment, (some say the eleventh.) See John xiii: 34. "A new commandment I give unto you, (what is it, Lord?) that ye love one another." And also xx: 12. The other is to love our neighbor as ourself. John says: "And this commandment have we from him (Christ,) that he who loveth God loveth his brother [Pg 22]also." John iv: 21, and ii: 8-11. In his letter to the Ephesians he says: "Having abolished in his flesh the *enmity* even the law of commandments contained in ordinances." ii: 15. See the reverse. vi: 2. To the Colossians he asks, "Why as though living in the world, are ye subject to ordinances where all are to perish with their using?" And says: "Touch not, taste not, handle not." (Does Paul here teach us to forsake the ordinances of God, instituted by the Saviour—Baptism and the Lord's Supper? Yes, just as clearly as he does to forsake the whole law.)

When writing to the Hebrews more than thirty years after the crucifixion, he calls these ordinances *carnal,* imposed on them (the Jews) until Christ our High Priest should come. ix: 10, 11. He also calls the law of commandments *carnal,* too, and says: "For there is verily a disannulling of the commandments going before, for the law made nothing perfect, but the bringing in of a better hope did." vii: 16, 18-19. "For when Moses had spoken *every precept* to all the people according to the *law* he took the blood of calves and of goats, with water, and scarlet wool, and hyssop, and sprinkled both the BOOK and all the people." ix: 19. Now we see clearly that the book of the law of Moses from which Paul has been quoting through the whole before mentioned epistles, is as distinctly separate from the tables of stone (or fleshly table of the heart,) as they were when deposited in the Ark thirty-three hundred years ago. Therefore we think that here is clear proof that he has kept up the distinction between the "handwriting of ordinances" (meaning Moses' own handwriting in his book,) and the "ten commandments written by the finger of God."

Let us now turn to the Epistle of James, said to be written more than twenty-five years after the law of ceremonies were nailed to the cross, and see if he does not teach us distinctly, that we are bound to keep the commandments given on tables of stone. He says, "the man that shall be a DOER of the *perfect law* of liberty shall be blessed in his deed." i: 25. "If ye fulfill the royal *law* according to the scripture, thou shalt love thy neighbor as thyself, ye do well." Why? Because the Saviour in quoting from the commandments, in answer to the Ruler, what he should do to inherit eternal life, taught the same doctrine. Matt. xix: 19. Further: "For whosoever shall keep the whole *law* and yet offend in one point, shall be guilty of *all.*" In the next verse he quotes from the [Pg 23]ten commandments again, namely, Adultery and Murder, (what the Saviour in the fifth chapter of Matt. calls the least, that is the smallest commandment,) and says if we commit them we become transgressors of the *law.* Of what *law*? Next verse says the *law of liberty* by which we are to be "judged." ii: 8, 11.

Now will it not be admitted by every reasonable person that James has included the whole of the ten commandments, by calling them the perfect law of liberty. 2d, "The royal *law* according to the scripture," and 3d, "the *law of liberty* by which we are to be judged." (Royal relates to imperial and kingly.) Perfect means COMPLETE, *entire,* the WHOLE. Then I understand James thus: This *law* emanated from the king, the Supreme Ruler of the universe, and to be perfect must be just what it was when it came from his hand, and that no *change* had, or could take place, (and remember now, this is more than twenty-five years since the ceremonies with the Jewish Sabbaths were nailed to the cross,) for the very best of reasons, until the judgment, because he shows that we are to be judged by *that law.* Then I ask by what parity of reasoning any one can make the law of the ten commandments perfect, while they at the same time assert that the fourth one is abolished? and that on no better evidence than calling it the JEWISH Sabbath. Now let us look at the Apostle John's testimony.

"And hereby we do know that we know him if we keep his commandments. He that saith I know him and keepeth not his commandments is a LIAR, and the truth is not in him." Now no man, more especially one who professes to abide by the whole truth, feels entirely easy if he is called a *liar*. Now John please explain yourself. Hear him: "Brethren, I write no new commandment unto you but an *old* commandment which ye had from the beginning. The old commandment is the *word* which ye have heard from theBEGINNING." What do you mean by *beginning*? Turn to my Gospel, 1st ch. "In the *beginning* was the word,"—"the same was in the *beginning* with God." 1, 2. See Gen. i ch.: "In the *beginning* God created the heavens and the earth." Then you are pointing us to the seventh day of creation, in which God instituted the seventh day Sabbath of rest, for the *old* commandment in the *beginning*. ii: 3. Certainly there is no other place to point to. Does not Jesus point us to the same place for the *beginning* when marriage was first instituted. Matt. xix: 4. [Pg 24]In my second letter to the church, I have taught the same doctrine: viz. "This is the commandment that as ye have heard from the *beginning ye should walk in it.*" (practice it.) ii: 5, 6. "A *new* commandment I write unto you." 7th v. This is the one that Jesus gave us on that memorable night in which he was betrayed, after he had instituted the sacrament and washed our feet. He said "By this shall all men know that ye are my disciples if ye have love one to another." xiii: 34, 35. The first then teaches us, Love to God, 2d, to Love our neighbor as ourself; "on these two commandments (says Jesus) hang all the law and the prophets." Then we understand this is the essence of the ten commandments, and if we do not keep the Sabbath we do not love God. Jesus says, "If ye love me ye will keep my commandments." We are repeatedly told that the Sabbath was changed or forever abolished, at the crucifiction of our Lord, and it is stated by the most competent authorities that John wrote this epistle about sixty years afterwards, and that about six years after this our blessed Lord revealed to him the state of the Church down to the judgment of the great day. In the xiv ch. Rev. 6-11, he saw three angels following each other in succession: first one preaching the everlasting gospel (second advent doctrine); 2d, announcing the fall of Babylon; 3d, calling God's people out of her by showing the awful destruction that awaited all such as did not obey. He sees the separation and cries out, "Here is the patients of the Saints, here are they that keep the *commandments* of God and the faith of Jesus." And this picture was so deeply impressed on his mind, that when the Saviour said to him "Behold I come quickly and my reward is with me," he seemed to understand this, saying—"Blessed are they that *do* his commandments that they may have right to the tree of life, and may enter in through the gates into the city." xxii: 14. Now it seems to me that the seventh day Sabbath is more clearly included in these commandments, than thou shalt not steal, nor kill, nor commit adultery, for it is the only one that was written at the creation or in the*beginning*. He allows no stopping place this side of the gates of the city. Then, if we do not keep that day, John has made out his case, that we are all *liars*. We say in every other case the type must be continued until it is superseded by the antitype, as in the case of the passover, until our Lord was crucified. So then, as Paul tells us, "there remaineth a keeping of the Sabbath to the people of God," and that we believe will be in the Milenium, [Pg 25]the seven thousandth year, so that the seventh day Sabbath and no other will answer for the type, and those who keep the first or the eighth day Sabbath cannot consistently look for the antitype of rest or the great Sabbath, short of one thousand years in the future.

Again: Isaiah says: "To the law and to the testimony if they speak not according to this word, it is because there is no light in them." viii: 20. Now if the Gentiles are under no law, as 'is asserted,' pray tell me what right, as Gentiles, have we to appeal to the law and testimony, or to this text.

In the xxiv. of Matt. our Saviour says to his disciples, in answer to their questions, When shall these things be? and what shall be the sign of thy coming, and the end of the world? "When ye therefore shall see the abomination of desolation spoken of by Daniel the prophet, stand in the holy place," &c. 15v. "Pray ye that your flight be not in the winter, neither on the Sabbath day." 20v. The first question is, at what age of the world is this, where our Lord recognizes the Sabbath? 1st. It is agreed on all hands that this time to which he here refers, never transpired until the destruction of Jerusalem in A.D. 70, about forty years after his crucifiction. 2d. Some others say, down to the second Advent! The first mentioned is safe ground and sufficient for our purpose; nor need we stop to inquire why our Lord gave these directions, it is forever settled that he directed the minds of his followers to THE, not *a* Sabbath. Keep it in remembrance, that he told the Pharisees that he was Lord, not of *a*, but of THE Sabbath, meaning that one which of course had already been established. The 2d question is, did our Lord ever trifle with, or mislead his disciples? The response is No! Then it is clear that if he taught them to pray at all, it must be in faith, and he of course would hear them and mediate with the Father to change the day of their flight. I ask what kind of a prayer and with what kind of faith would his disciples have asked to have this day changed, if as we are told, it was abolished some forty years before, and they had, contrary to the will of God, persisted in keeping up this seventh day Sabbath. Any one who has confidence in God's word, knows that such a prayer never would be answered. What if you do say the Jews always kept that Sabbath, and it was the same seventh day Sabbath which they kept when he was teaching them in their synagogues? I, say so too! (and that fact will be presented by and by, in its place.) This does not touch the point. Jesus was here giving instructions to his [Pg 26]followers, both Jew and Gentile, respecting *the* Sabbath which they would have to do with. It is immaterial what kind of sophistry is presented to overthrow the point, nothing can touch it short of proving it a mistranslation. Jesus did here recognize the perpetuity of the *seventh day Sabbath*. And John will continue to make all men liars that say they know him and refuse the light presented and disregard this commandment. If God instituted the Sabbath in Paradise and has not abolished it here, then must it be *perpetual?* If Paul's argument in iii. Rom. that the law is established through faith, is correct then is it *perpetual*. If James' royal *perfect law* of liberty, which we are to be doers of, and judged by, means the commandments, then is the Sabbath *perpetual*. If the Apostle John has made out a clear case, by citing us back to the *beginning* of creation, and by *walking* in and doing these commandments, we shall have right to the tree of life and enter in by the gates into the city; then it *must be perpetual*. If the earthly Sabbath is typical of the heavenly, then must it be *perpetual*. If not one jot or one tittle can ever pass from the law, then must it be *perpetual*. If the Saviour, in answer to the young man who asked him what he should do to inherit *eternal life*, gave a safe direction for Gentiles to follow, viz: "If thou wilt enter into *life* keep the commandments (and these included those commandments which his Father had given), then, without *contradiction* the Sabbath is *perpetual*, and all the arguments which ever can be presented against the fourth commandment being observed before God wrote it on tables of stone to prove that it is not binding on Gentiles, falls powerless before this one sentence: *If thou wilt enter into life, keep the commandments.* I say the proof is positive that the Sabbath was a constituent part of the commandments, and Jesus says the Sabbath 'was made for man.' The Jews were only a *fragment of creation*.

"The principle is settled in all governments that there are but two ways in which any law can cease to be binding upon the people. It may expire by its own limitations, or it may be repealed by the same authority which enacted it; and in the latter case the repealing act must be as explicit as that by which the obligation was originally imposed." Now we have it in proof that the Sabbath was instituted in Paradise, the *first* of all laws without any limitation, and no enactment by God to abolish it, unless what we have already referred to can be considered proof. One more passage which I have not alluded to will show that it was not [Pg 27]abolished at the crucifiction, for his disciples kept the Sabbath while he was resting in his tomb. See Luke xxiii: 55, 56. Let us now pass to another part of the subject. The third question:

WAS THE SEVENTH-DAY SABBATH EVER CHANGED? IF SO, WHEN, AND FOR WHAT REASON?

Here we come to a question which has more or less engaged the attention of the whole christian world, and the greater portion of those who believe in a crucified Saviour say that this change took place, and is dated from his resurrection. Some say subsequently, while a minority insist upon it that there is no proof for the change. Now to obtain the truth and nothing but the truth on this important subject, I propose to present, or quote from standard authors on both sides of the question, and try the whole by the standard of divine truth. 1st. Buck's Theological Dictionary, to which no doubt thousands of ministers and laymen appeal to sustain their argument for the change, says: "Under the christian dispensation the Sabbath is *altered* from the *seventh* to the *first day* of the week." The arguments for the change, are these: 1st. "The *seventh* day was observed by the Jewish church in memory of the rest of God; so the *first* day of the week has always been observed by the christian church in memory of *Christ's resurrection.* 2d. Christ made repeated visits to his disciples on that day. 3d. It is called the Lord's day. Rev. i: 10. 4th. On this day the Apostles were assembled, when the Holy Ghost came down so visibly upon them to qualify them for the conversion of the world. 5th. On this day we find Paul at Troas when the disciples came together to break bread. 6th. The directions the Apostles gave to Christians plainly alludes to their assembling on that day. 7th. Pliny bears witness of the first day of the week being kept as a festival in honor of the resurrection of Christ."

"Numerous have been the days appointed by man for religious services, but these are not binding because of *human* institution. Not so the Sabbath. It is of *divine* institution, so it is to be kept holy unto the Lord."

Doct. Dodridge, whose ability and piety has seldom or rarely been disputed, comments on some of the above articles thus: (Commentary p. 606.) "Upon the first day of the week let every one of you lay by him in store, as God hath prospered him, that there be no gatherings when I come." 1 Cor. xvi: 2. "Show that it was to be put into a [Pg 28]common stock. The argument drawn from hence for the religious observance of the first day of the week in these primitive churches of Corinth and Galacia is too *obvious* to need any further illustration, and yet too important to be passed by in entire silence." Again, p. 904, "I was in the spirit on the Lord's day," &c. Rev. i: 10. "It is so very unnatural and contrary to the use of the word in all other authors to interpret this of the Jewish Sabbath, as Mr. Baxter justly argues at large, that I cannot but conclude with him and the generality of Christian writers on this subject, that this text *strongly* infers the extraordinary regard paid to the first day of the week in the Apostle's time as a day solemnly consecrated to Christ in memory of his resurrection from the dead." There is much more, but these are his strong arguments. I shall quote some more from the Commentaries by and by. I wish to place by the side of these arguments one from the British Quarterly Theological Review and Ecclesiastical Recorder, of Jan. 1830, which I extract from 'the *Institution of the Sabbath day,*' by Wm. Logan Fisher, of Philadelphia, a book in which there is much valuable information on this subject, though I disagree with the writer, because his whole labor is to abolish the Sabbath; yet he gives much light on this subject, from which I take the liberty to make some quotations.

But to the Quarterly Review of 1830: "It is said that the observance of the seventh day Sabbath is transferred in the Christian church to the first day of the week. We ask by what authority, and are very much mistaken if an examination of all the texts of the New Testament, in which the first day of the week or Lord's day is mentioned, does not prove that there is no divine or Apostolic precept enjoining its observance, nor any certain evidence from scripture that it was, in fact, so observed in the times of the Apostles. Accordingly we search the scriptures in vain, either for an Apostolic precept, appointing the first day of the week to be observed in the place of the Jewish Sabbath, or for any unequivocal proof that the first christians so observed it—there are only three or, at most four places of scripture, in which the first day of the week is mentioned. The next passage is in Acts xx: 7. 'Upon the first day of the week when the disciples came together to break bread, Paul preached unto them.' All that St. Luke here tells us plainly is, that on a particular occasion the christians of Troas met together on the first day of the week to celebrate the Eucharist and to hear Paul preach. This is the only place in [Pg 29]scripture, in which the first day of the week is in any way connected with any acts of public worship, and he who would certainly infer from this *solitary instance* that the first day of every week was consecrated by the Apostles to religious purposes, must be far gone in the art of drawing universal conclusion from particular premises."

On page 178, Mr. Fisher says, "I have examined several different translations of the scriptures, both from the Hebrew and the Septuagint, with notes and anotations more extensive than the texts; have traced as far as my leisure would permit, various ecclesiastical histories, some of them voluminous and of ancient date; have paid considerable attention to the writings of the earliest authors in the christian era, and to rare works, old and of difficult access, which treat upon this subject; I have read with care many of the publications of sectarians to sustain the institution; I have omitted nothing within my reach, and I have found not one shred of argument, or authority of any kind, that may not be deemed of partial and sectarian character, to support the institution of the first day of the week as a day of peculiar holiness. But, in the place of argument, I have found opinions without number—volumes filled with idle words that have no truth in them. In the want of texts of scripture, I have found perversions; in the want of truth, false statements. I have seen it stated that Justin Marter in his apology, speaks of Sunday as a holy day; that Eusebius, bishop of Cesarea, who lived in the fourth century, establishes the fact of the transfer of the *seventh* to the first day, by Christ himself. These things are *not true*. These authors say no such thing. I have seen other early authors referred to as establishing the same point, but they are equally false."

Here then is the testimony of four authors, two for the change and two against it, from the old and new world. No truth seeking, unbiased mind can hesitate for a moment on which side to decide, after comparing them with the inspired word.

Doctor JENKS of Boston, author of the Comprehensive Commentary, (purporting to comprehend *all* other commentators on the bible,) after quoting author after author, on this subject, ventures forth with *his* unsupported opinion in these words: "Here is a Christian Sabbath observed by the disciples and *owned by our Lord*. The visit Christ made to his disciples was on the first day of the week, and the first day of the week is the only day of the week or month or year ever mentioned by numbers in all the New [Pg 30]Testament, and that is several times spoken of as a day *religiously* observed." Where? Echo answers, where!

HEMAN HUMPHREY, President of Amherst College, from whose book I have already made some quotations, after devoting some thirty-four pages to the establishment and perpetuation of the seventh day Sabbath, comes to his fourth question, viz. 'Has the day been changed?' Singular as this question may appear by the side of what he had already written to establish and perpetuate the seventh day Sabbath from the seventh day of creation down to the resurrection of the just, but as every man feels that it his privilege to justify and explain, when precept and practice does not agree—so is it with President Humphrey, he can now shape the scriptures to suit every one that has followed in the wake of Pope Gregory for 1225 years. He says, "The fourth commandment is so expressed as to admit of a change in the day,"—thus striking vitally every argument he had before presented. Hear him—he says the seventh day is the Sabbath; "it was so at that time, (in the beginning) and for many ages after, but it is not said, that it always *shall be*—it is the *Sabbath* day which we are to remember; and so at the close, it is the *Sabbath* which was hallowed and blessed and not the *seventh* day. The Sabbath then, the holy rest itself, is one thing. The day on which we are to rest is another." I ask, in the name of common sense, how we should know how or when to keep the Sabbath if it did not matter which day. If the President could not see the sanctification of the seventh day in the decalogue what did he mean by quoting Gen. ii: 3, so often, where it says "*God blessed the seventh day and sanctified it.*"

Again, he says "Redemption is a greater work than creation, hence the change." Fifthly, God early consecrated the Christian Sabbath by a most remarkable outpouring of his spirit at the day of Pentecost. And that Jesus has left us his own example by not saying a syllable after his resurrection about keeping the *Jewish Sabbath*. He also quotes the four passages about Jesus and his disciples keeping the first day of the week. Here, he says, the inference to our minds is *irresistible*—for keeping the first day of the week instead of the *seventh*. And further says, "it might be proved by innumerable quotations from the writings of the Apostolic Fathers," &c. All this may be very true in itself, but it all falls to the ground for the want of one single precept from the bible. If Redemption, because it was greater than Creation, and the remarkable display of God's power at the [Pg 31]Pentecost, and Christ never saying any thing about the *Jewish Sabbath* after his resurrection are such *strong* proofs that the perpetual seventh day Sabbath was changed to the first day at that time, and must be believed because learned men say so, what shall we do with the sixth day, on which our blessed Saviour expired on the cross; darkness for three hours had covered the earth, and the vail of the Temple was rent from top to the bottom, and there was such an earthquake throughout vast creation that we have only to open our eyes and look at the rent rocks for a clear and perfect demonstration that this whole globe was shaken from centre to circumference, and the graves of the dead were opened. Matt. xxvii: 50, 53. You may answer me that Popery has honored that day by calling it good Friday, and the next first day following Easter Sunday, &c., but after all, nothing short of bible argument will satisfy the earnest inquirer after truth. The President had already shown that the *Jewish* Sabbath was abolished at Christ's death. What reason then had he to believe that the Saviour would speak of it afterwards. So also the Pentecost had been a type from the giving the law at Sinai to be kept annually for about 1500 years, consequently it would be solemnized on every day of the week, at each revolving year, as is the case with the 4th of July: three years ago it was on the fourth day and now it comes on the seventh day of the week. Further, see Peter standing amidst the amazed multitude, giving the scripture reason for this miraculous display of God's power. He does not give the most distant hint that this was, or was to be, the day of the week for worship, or the true Sabbath, neither do any of the Apostles then, or afterwards, for when they kept this day the next year, it must have been the second day of the week. We must have better evidence than what has been adduced, to believe this was the Sabbath, for according to the type, seven Sabbaths were to be complete, (and there was no other way given them to come to the right day,) from the day they kept the first, or from the resurrection. Here then is proof positive that the Sabbath in this year was the day before the Pentecost. See Luke xxiii: 55, 56. If President H. is right, then was there two Sabbaths to be kept in succession in one week. Where is the precept? No where! Well, says the inquirer, I want to see the bible proof for this '*Christian Sabbath observed by the disciples, and owned by our Lord.*' W. Jenks. Here it will be necessary for us to understand, first how God has computed time. In Gen. i. we read, "And [Pg 32]God said let there be lights in the firmament of the heaven, to divide the day from the night, and let them be for signs and for seasons and for days and years." 14 v. 16 v. says, "the greater light to rule the day,"—from sunrise to sunset. Now there are many modes invented for computing time. We say our day begins at 12 o'clock at night; seamen begin theirs twelve hours sooner, at noon; the Jews commence their days at 6 o'clock in the evening, between the two extremes. Are we *all* right? No! Who shall settle this question? God! Very well: He called the light day, and the darkness he called night, and the evening and the morning were the first day. Gen. i: 5. Then the twenty-four hour day commenced at 6 o'clock in the evening. How is that, says one? Because you cannot regulate the day and night to have what the Saviour calls twelve hours in the day, without establishing the time from the centre of the earth, the equator, where, at the beginning of the sacred year, the sun rises and sets at 6 o'clock. At *this* time, while the sun is at the summer solstice, the inhabitants of the north pole have no night, while at this same time at the south it is about all night, therefore the inhabitants of the earth have no other right time to commence their twenty-four hour day, than beginning at 6 o'clock in the evening. God said to Moses '*from even, unto even, shall you celebrate your Sabbath.*' Then of course the next day must begin where the Sabbath ended. History shows that the Jews obeyed and commenced their days at 6 o'clock in the evening. Now then we will try to investigate the main argument by which these authors, and thousands of others say the Sabbath was changed. The first is in John xx: 19, "Then the same day at evening, being the first day of the week when the doors where shut where the disciples were assembled *for fear of the Jews* (mark it) came Jesus and stood in their midst, and said peace be unto you." Here we understand this to be the same day of the resurrection. On that same day he travelled with the two disciples to Emans, sixty furlongs (7-1/2 miles), and they constrained him to abide with them, for it was toward evening and the *day was far spent.* Luke xxiv: 29. After this the disciples travelled the 7-1/2 miles back to Jerusalem and soon after they found the disciples, the Saviour, as above stated, was in their midst. Now it cannot be disputed but what this was the evening after the resurrection, for Jesus rose in the morning, some ten or eleven hours after the first day had commenced. Then the evening of the first day was passing away, and therefore the evening brought to view in [Pg 33]the text was the close of the first day or the commencing of the second. McKnight's translation says, "in the evening of that day." Purver's translation says, "the evening of that day on the first after the Sabbath." Further, wherever the phrase first day of the week, occurs in the New Testament, the word day is in *italics*, showing that it is not the original; but supplied by translators. Again, it is asserted that Jesus met with his disciples the next first day. See 26v: "And *after* eight days again his disciples were within, and Thomas with them, then came Jesus, the doors being shut, and stood in the midst, and said peace be unto you." Dr. Adam Clark in referring to this 26v, says: "It seems likely that this was precisely on that day se'night on which Christ had appeared to them before; and from this we may learn that this was the weekly meeting of the Apostles." Now it appears to me that a little child, with the simple rules of addition and subtraction, could have refuted this man. I feel astonished that men who profess to be ambassadors for God do not expose such downright perversion of scripture, but it may look clear to those who want to have it so. Not many months since, in conversation with the Second Advent lecturer in New Bedford, I brought up this subject. He told me I did not understand it. See here, says he. I can make it plain, counting his fingers thus: Sunday, Monday, Tuesday, Wednesday, Thursday, Friday, Saturday, Sunday—does'nt that make eight days after? and because I would not concede, he parted from me as one that was obstinate and self-willed. Afterwards musing on the subject, I said, this must be the way then to understand it: *Count Sunday Twice.* If any of them were to be paid for eight days labor, they would detect the error in a moment if their employer should attempt to put the first and last days together, and offer them pay but for seven. Eight days *after* the evening of the first day would stand thus: The second day of the week would certainly be the first of the eight. Then to count eight days of twenty-four hours *after,* we must begin at the close of the evening of the first, and count to the close of the evening of the second day; to where the Jews (by God's command) commenced their third day. But suppose we calculate it by our mode of keeping time. Our Lord appears to his disciples the first time at the close of Sunday evening. Now count eight days *after,* (with your fingers or anything else,) and it will bring you to Monday evening. Now I ask if this looks like Sunday, the first day of the week?

[Pg 34]

Father Miller also gives his reasons for the change, in his lecture on the great Sabbath: "One is Christ's resurrection and his often meeting with his disciples *afterwards* on that day. This, with the example of the Apostles, is strong evidence that the proper creation Sabbath to man, came on the first day of the week." His proof is this: "Adam must have rested on the first day of his life, and thus you will see that to Adam it was the first day of the week, for it would not be reasonable to suppose that Adam began to reckon time before he was created." He certainly could not be able to work six days before the first Sabbath. And thus with the second Adam; the first day of the week he arose and lived. And we find by the *bible* and by history, that the first day of the week "*was ever afterwards observed as a day of worship.*" Now I say there is no more truth in these assertions, than there is in those I have already quoted. There is not one passage in the bible to show that Christ met with his disciples on the first day of the week after the day of his resurrection, nor that the first day of the week was *ever afterwards* observed as a day of worship; save only in one instance, and that shall be noticed in its place. And it seems to me if Adam could not reckon time only from his creation then by the same rule no other man could reckon time before his birth, and by this showing Christ could not reckon his time until after his resurrection. It is painful to me to expose the errors of one whom I have so long venerated, and still love for the flood of light he has given the world in respect to the Second Advent of our Saviour; but God's word must be vindicated if we have to cut off a right arm, "there is nothing true but truth!" I pray God to forgive him in joining the great multitude of Advent believers, to sound the retreat back beyond the *tarrying* time, just when the virgins had gained a glorious victory over the world, the flesh, and the devil! Go back from this to the slumbering quarters now; nothing but treachery to our Master's cause ever dictated such a course! I never can be made to believe that our glorious Commander designed that we should leave our sacrifices smoking on the altar of God, in the midst of the enemies' land, but rather that we should be pushing onward from victory to victory, until we are established in the Capital of *His* kingdom. Would it have been expedient or a mark of courage in General Taylor, after he had conquered the Mexican army on the 9th May last, to have retreated back to the capital of the U. States, to place himself and army on the *broad platform* of liberty, and [Pg 35]commence to travel the ground over again for the purpose of pursuing and overcoming his vanquished foe? No! Every person of common sense knows that such a course would have overwhelmed him and all his followers with unutterable disgrace, no matter how unrighteous the contest. Not so with this, for our cause is one of the most glorious, tho' it be the most trying that ever the sun shone upon since God placed it in the heavens. Onward and victory, then, are our watchwords, and no retreating back to, or beyond the cry at *Midnight!* But to the subject. Did our Saviour ever meet with his disciples on the first day of the week after the evening of the day of his resurrection? The xxi. ch. John says "they went a fishing, and while there Jesus appeared unto them." In the 14th v. he says, "This is now the third time that Jesus shewed himself to his disciples after that he was risen from the dead." Now turn to 1 Cor. xv: 4-7: Paul's testimony is, 'that he was seen of Cephas, then of the twelve, after that of above five hundred brethren at once, and then of James, then of all the Apostles.' These are all that are specified, up to his going into heaven. Now pray tell me if you can, where these men got their information respecting the frequent meetings on the first day of the week. The bible says no such thing. But let us pursue the subject and look at the third text, "Upon the first day of the week let every one of you lay by him in *store*, as God has prospered him, that there be no gatherings when I come." Now please turn back to Dr. Dodridge's authority, he says the argument is too obvious to need any illustration, that the money was put into common stock, and that this was the religious observance of the first day of the week. Now whoever will read the first six verses of this chapter, and compare them with Rom. xv: 26-33, will see that Paul's design was to collect some money for the poor saints at Jerusalem, and their laying it by them in store until he came that way; for it plainly implies that they were at home, for no one could understand that you had money lying by you in store, if it was in common stock or in other hands. Again, see Acts xviii: 4, 11. Paul preaching every Sabbath day, at this very time, for eighteen months, to these very same Corinthians, bids them farewell, to go up to the feast at Jerusalem, 21 v. By reading to xxi. ch. 17 v. you have his history until he arrives there. Now I ask, if Dr. Dodridge's clear illustration can or will be relied on, when Luke clearly teaches that Paul's *manner* was, and that he did always preach to them on the Sabbath, which, of course, [Pg 36]was the Seventh day, and not the first day of the week. Fourth text, John says: I was in the spirit on the Lord's day. Here Dr. D. concludes with the generality of christian writers on this subject that this strongly infers the extraordinary regard paid to the first day of the week, as solemnly consecrated to Christ, &c. If the scripture any where called this the Lord's day, there might be some reason to believe their statements, but the seventh day Sabbath is called the Lord's day. See Exod. xx: 10.

Mr. Fisher, in speaking of the late Harrisburg convention of 1844-45, says, "The most spirited debate that occurred at the assembly was to fix a proper name for the first day of the week, whether it should be called *Sabbath*, the *Christian* Sabbath or *Lord's* day. The reason for this dispute was, that there was no authority for calling the first day of the week by either one of these names. To pretend that that command was fixed and unchangeable, and yet to alter it to please the fancy of man, is in itself ridiculous. It is hardly possible in the nature of man, that a class of society should be receiving pay for their services and not be influenced thereby:—in the nature of things they will avoid such doctrines as are repugnant to them that give them bread."

Now we come to the fifth and last, and only one spoken of in all the New Testament, for a meeting on the first day of the week. Luke says, "Upon the first day of the week when the disciples came together to break bread, Paul preached unto them, *ready to depart on the morrow*: and continued his speech until midnight." Acts xx: 7. Now by following the scripture mode of computing time, from 6 o'clock in the evening to 6 o'clock in the morning, as has been shown, Paul to commence on the beginning of the first day would begin on what we call Saturday evening at 6 o'clock, and preach till midnight. After that he restores to life the young man, then breaks bread and talked till the break of day, which would be Sunday morning. Then he commenced his journey for Jerusalem and travelled and sailed all day Sunday, the first day of the week, and two other days in succession. xx: 11-15. Now it seems to me, if Paul did teach or keep the first day of the week for the Sabbath or a holy day, he violated the sanctity of it to all intents and purposes, without giving one single reason for it; all the proof presented here is a night meeting. Please see the quotation from the British Quarterly Review. But let us look at it the way in which *we* compute time: I think it will be fair to premise, that about midnight was the middle of [Pg 37]Paul's meeting; at any rate there is but one midnight to a twenty-four hour day. We say that Sunday, the first day of the week, does not commence until 12 o'clock Saturday night. Then it is very clear, if he is preaching on the first day till midnight, according to our reckoning it must be on Sunday night, and his celebrating the Lord's supper after midnight would make it that he broke bread on *Monday, the second day*, and that the day time on Sunday is not included, unless he had continued his speech through the day till midnight. Now the text says that on the first day of the week they came together to break bread. To *prove that they did break bread on that day*, we must take the mode in which the Jews computed time, and allow the first day of the week to begin at 6 o'clock on Saturday evening, and to follow Paul's example, pay no regard to the first day, after daylight, but to travel, &c. If *our* mode of time is taken, they broke bread on the second day, and that would destroy the meaning of the text. Here then, in this text, is the *only* argument that can be adduced in the scriptures of divine truth, for a *change of the perpetual seventh day* Sabbath of the Lord our God to the first day of the week.

Now I'll venture the assertion, that there is no law or commandment recorded in the bible, that God has held so sacred among men, as the keeping of His Sabbath. Where then, I ask, is the living man that dare stand before God and declare that here is the change for the church of God to keep the first instead of the seventh day of the week for the Sabbath. If it could be proved that Paul preached here all of the first day, the only inference that could be drawn, would be, to break bread on that day!

There is one more point worthy of our attention, that is, the teaching and example of Jesus. I have been told by one that is looked up to as a strong believer in the second coming of the Lord this fall, that Jesus broke the Sabbath. Jesus says, I have kept my Father's commandments. It is said that he 'broke the Sabbath,' because he allowed his disciples to pluck the corn and eat it on that day, and the Pharisees condemned them. He says, "If ye had known what this meaneth, I will have mercy and not sacrifice, ye would not have condemned the *guiltless.*" Then they were not *guilty*. See Deut. xxiii: 25. He immediately cites them to David and his men, shewing that it was lawful and right when hungry, even to eat the shoe bread that belonged only to the priests, and told them that he was Lord of the Sabbath day. Here he shows too, that he was with his [Pg 38]disciples passing to the synagogue to teach; they ask him if it was lawful to heal on the Sabbath day. He asks them if they had a sheep fall into the ditch on the Sabbath, if they would not haul him out? How much better then is a man than a sheep? Wherefore it is lawful to do well on the Sabbath days; and immediately healed the man with a withered hand. Matt. xii: 1-13. On another Sabbath day, while he was teaching, he healed a woman that had been bound of satan eighteen years, and when the ruler of the synagogue began to find fault, he called him a hypocrite, and said "doth not each one of you on the Sabbath day loose his ox or his ass from the stall and lead him away to watering; and all his adversaries were *ashamed.*" Luke xiii: 10-17. The xiv. chapter of Luke is quoted to prove that he broke the Sabbath because he went into the Pharisees house with many others on the Sabbath day to eat bread. Here he saw a man with the dropsy and he asked them if it was lawful to heal on the Sabbath day. 'And they held their peace and he took him and healed him,' and asked them 'which of them having an ox or an ass fall into the pit, would not straitway pull him out on the Sabbath day; and they could not answer him again.' 1-6 v. And 'he continued to teach them, by showing them when they made a feast to call the poor, the maimed, the lame, the blind, and then they should be blessed.' Read the chapter, and you will readily see that he took this occasion, as the most befitting, to teach them by parables, what their duty was at weddings and feasts, in the same manner as he taught them in their synagogues.

There is still another passage, and I believe the only one, to which reference has been made, (except where he opened the eyes of a man that was born blind,) for proof that he broke the Sabbath. It is recorded in John v: 5-17. Here Jesus found a man that had been sick thirty-eight years, by the pool of Bethesda, 'he saith unto him rise, take up thy bed and walk,—therefore did they persecute Jesus and sought to slay him, because he had done these things on the Sabbath day.' 16 v. 'But Jesus answered them, my Father worketh hitherto and I work.' If they did not work every hour and moment of time, it would be impossible for man to exist: Here undoubtedly he had reference to these and other acts of necessity and mercy; but the great sin for which professors in this enlightened age charge the Saviour with in this transaction, is, in directing the man to take up his bed, contrary to law. It is clear the people [Pg 39]were forbidden to carry burthens on the Sabbath day, as in Jer. xvii: 21, 22, but by reading the 24th v. in connection with Neh. xiii: 15-22, we learn that this prohibition related to what was lawful for them to do on the other six days of the week, viz. merchandise and trading. See proof, Neh. x: 31: also unlawful, as in Amos viii: 5. We need not, nor we cannot misunderstand the fourth commandment, taken in connection with the other nine, they were simple and pure written by the finger of God; but in the days of our Saviour it had become heavily laden with Jewish traditions, hence when Jesus appeals to them whether it is lawful to do good and to heal on the Sabbath days, their mouths are closed because they cannot contradict him from the law nor the prophets. The Saviour no where interferes with them in their most rigid observance of the day; but when they find fault with him for performing his miracles of mercy on that day, he tells them they have broken the law; and in another place, "If a man on the Sabbath day receive circumcision without breaking the law of Moses, are ye angry at me because I have made a man every whit whole on the Sabbath day?" He then says, "Judge not according to the appearance, but judge righteous judgment." vii: 23, 24. Did he break the Sabbath? Now the law requires that the beasts shall rest; but what is the practice of many of those who are the most strict in keeping Sunday for the Sabbath. Sick, or well, ministers or laymen, do they not ride back and forth to meeting? Again, is it right and lawful to carry forth our dead on the Sabbath? or carry the communion service back and forth. The Apostle says, 'believe and be baptized.' Suppose this should be on the Sabbath and we were some distance from the water, would any one interfere with us if we carried our change of apparel with us and back again, or have we in so doing transgressed the law; if we have, it is high time we made a full stop. Jesus undoubtedly had good reasons for directing the sick man to take up his bed and walk, but I cannot learn that he justified any one else in carrying their bed on the Sabbath, unless in a case of necessity and mercy, such as he cited them to, as watering their cattle, and pulling them out of the ditch, and eating when hungry, and being healed when sick. Be it also remembered that when the Sanhedrim tried him they did not condemn him, as in the other cases cited; so in this, they failed for want of scripture testimony. He was the Lord of the Sabbath, and the law of ceremonies were now about[Pg 40]to cease forever, the ten commandments with the keeping of the Sabbath therefore were to be stripped of these ceremonies and all of their traditions, and left as pure to be written on the hearts of the Gentiles as when first written on tables of stone, therefore Jesus taught that it was right to do good on the Sabbath day, and whoever follows his example and teaching will keep the seventh day Sabbath holy and acceptable to God. They will also judge righteous judgement, and not according to appearance.

There is but one Christian Sabbath named, or established in the bible, and that individual, whoever he is, that undertakes to abolish or change it, is the *real Sabbath breaker.* Remember that the keeping the commandments is the only safe guide through the gates into the city.

My friends and neighbors, and especially my family, know that I have for more than twenty years, strictly endeavored to keep the first day of the week for the Sabbath, and I can say that I did it in all good conscience before God, on the ocean, and in foreign countries as well as my own, until about sixteen months since I read an article published in the Hope of Israel, by a worthy brother, T. M. Preble, of Nashua, which when I read and compared with the bible, convinced me that there never had been any change. Therefore the seventh day was the Sabbath, and God required me as well as him to keep it holy. Many things now troubled my mind as to how I could make this great change, family, friends, and brethren and, but this one passage of Scripture was, and always will be as clear as a sunbeam. "*What is that to thee: follow thou me.*" In a few days my mind was made up to begin to keep the fourth commandment, and I bless God for the clear light he has shed upon my mind in answer to prayer and a thorough examination of the scriptures on this great subject. Contrary views did, after a little, shake my position some, but I feel now that there is no argument nor sophistry that can becloud my mind again this side of the gates of the Holy City. Brother Marsh, who no doubt thinks, and perhaps thousands besides, that his paper is what it purports to be, THE VOICE OF TRUTH, takes the ground with the infidel that there is no Sabbath. Brother S. S. Snow, of New York, late editor of the Jubilee Standard, publishes to the world that he is the Elijah, preceding the advent of our Saviour, restoring all things: (the seventh day Sabbath must be one of the all things,) and yet he takes the same ground with

Br. Marsh, that the Sabbath[Pg 41]is forever abolished. As the seventh day Sabbath is a real prophecy, a picture (and not a shadow like the Jewish Sabbaths,) of the thing typified which is to come, I cannot see how those who believe in the change or abolition of the type, can have any confidence to look to God for the great antetype, the Sabbath of rest, to come to them.

Brother J. B. Cook has written a short piece in his excellent paper, the ADVENT TESTIMONY. It was pointed and good, but too short; and as brother Preble's Tract now before me, did not embrace the arguments which have been presented since he published it, it appeared to me that something was called for in this time of falling back from this great subject. I therefore present this book, hoping at least, that it will help to strengthen and save all honest souls seeking after truth.

A WORD RESPECTING THE HISTORY. At the close of the first century a controversy arose, whether both days should be kept or only one, which continued until the reign of Constantine the Great. By his laws, made in A. D. 321, it was decreed for the future that Sunday should be kept a day of rest in all the cities and towns; but he allowed the country people to follow husbandry. History further informs us that Constantine murdered his two sisters husbands and son, and his own familiar friend, that same year, and the year before boiled his wife in a cauldron of oil.—The controversy still continued down to A. D. 603, when Pope Gregory passed a law abolishing the seventh day Sabbath, and establishing the first day of the week. See Baronius Councils, 603. Barnfield's Eng. page 116, states that the Parliament of England met on Sundays till the time of Richard II. The first law of England made for keeping of Sunday, was in the time of Edward IV. about 1470. As these two books are not within my reach, I have extracted from T. M. Preble's tract on the Sabbath. Mr. Fisher says, it was Dr. Bound one of the rigid puritans, who applied the name *Sabbath* to the first day of the week, about the year 1795. "The word Sunday is not found in the bible," it derived its name from the heathen nations of the North, because the day was dedicated to the sun. Neither is the Sabbath applied to the first day any more than it is to the sixth day of the week. While Daniel beheld the little horn, (popery) he said, among other things, he would *think* to change times and laws. Now this could not mean of men, because it ever has been the prerogative of absolute rulers like himself, to change [Pg 42]manmade laws. Then to make the prophecy harmonize with the scripture, he must have meant times and laws established by God, because he might think and pass decrees as he has done, but he, nor all the universe could ever change God's times and laws. Jesus says that "times and seasons were in the power of the father." The Sabbath is the most important law which God ever instituted. "How long refuse ye to keep my commandments, and my laws, see for that the Lord hath given you the Sabbath." Exod. xvi: 28, 29. Then it's clear from the history, that this is in part what Daniel meant. Now the second advent believers have professed all confidence in his visions: why then doubt this. Whoever feels disposed to defend and sustain the decrees of that "blasphemous" power, and especially Pope Gregory and the great Constantine, the murderer, shown to be the *moral* reformer in this work of changing the Sabbath, are welcome to their principles and feelings. I detest these acts, in common with all others which have emanated from these ten and one horned powers. The Revelations show us clearly that they were originated by the devil. If you say this history is not true then you are bound to refute it. If you cannot, you are as much in duty bound to believe it as any other history, even, that George Washington died in 1799! If the bible argument, and testimony from history are to be relied on as evidence, then it is as clear as a sunbeam that the seventh day Sabbath is a perpetual sign, and is as binding upon man as it ever was. But we are told we must keep the first day of the week for the Sabbath as an ordinance to commemorate the resurrection of Jesus. I for one had rather believe Paul. See Rom. vi: 3-5; Gal. iii: 27; Col. ii: 12.

A word more respecting time. See 31st page. Here I have shown that the sun in the centre, regulates all time for the earth—fifty-two weeks to the year, one hundred and sixty-eight hours to the week, the seventh of which is twenty-four hours. Jesus says there are but twelve hours in the day, (from sunrise to sunset.) Then twelve hours night to make a twenty-four hour day, you see, must always begin at a certain period of time. No matter then whether the sun sets with us at eight in summer or 4 o'clk in winter. Now by this, and this is the scripture rule, days and weeks can, and most probably are, kept at the North and South polar regions. What an absurdity to believe that God does exonerate our fathers and brothers from[Pg 43]keeping his Sabbath while they are in these polar regions, fishing for seals and whales, should it be with them either all day or all night. If they have lost their reckoning of days and weeks, because there was, or was not any sun six months of the time, how could they learn what day of the week it was when they see the sun setting at 6 o'clock on the equator, if bound home from the South? By referring to Luke, xxiii ch. 55, 56, and xxiv: 1, we see that the people in Palestine had kept the days and weeks right from the creation; since which time, astronomers teach us that not even fifteen minutes have been lost. God does not require us to be any more exact in keeping time, than what we may or have learned from the above rules, but I am told there is a difference in time of twenty-four hours to the mariner that circumnavigates the globe. That, being true, is known to them, but it alters no time on the earth or sea.

But, says one, I should like to keep the Sabbath in *time*, just as Jesus did. Then you must live in Palestine, where their day begins seven hours earlier than ours; and yet it is at 6 o'clock in the evening the same period, though not the same by the sun, in which we begin our day. Let me illustrate: our earth, something in the form of an orange, is whirling over every twenty-four hours. It measures three hundred and sixty degrees, or about twenty-one thousand six hundred miles round, in the manner you would pass a string round an orange. Now divide this three hundred and sixty degrees by the twenty-four hour day, and the result is fifteen degrees, or nine hundred miles. Then every fifteen degrees we travel or sail eastward, the sun rises and sets one hour earlier in the period of the twenty-four hours: therefore those who live in Palestine, one hundred and seven degrees east of us, begins and closes the day seven hours earlier, so in proportion all the way round the globe, the sun always stationary! Then the Sabbath begins precisely at 6 o'clock on Friday evening, every where on this globe, and ends at the same period on what we call Saturday evening. God says 'every thing on its day,' 'from even unto even shall ye celebrate your Sabbath;' 'the evening and the morning was the first day.' He is an exact time keeper! I say then, in the name of all that is holy, heavenly and true, and as immortality is above all price, let us see to it that we are found fearing God and keeping his COMMANDMENTS, for this, we are taught, 'is the whole duty of man.' The proof is positive that the seventh day Sabbath is included in the commandments.

[Pg 44]
Bro. Marsh says, "Keeping the Sabbath is embraced in this covenant. Deut. v: 1-6, made with the children of Israel at Horeb. It was not made with their Fathers (the Patriarchs) but with us, even us, who are all ofUS HERE ALIVE THIS DAY. v. 3. This testimony first *negative*, he made it not with our Fathers, and then*positive* with *us*, is conclusive. Not a single proof can be presented from either the old or new testament, that it was instituted for any other people or nation." Now it is clear and positive that if the Sabbath is not binding on any other people than the Jews, by the same rule not one of the commandments is binding on any other people, who dare take such infidel ground? Was not the second covenant written on the hearts of the Gentile, even the law of Commandments? which Paul says 'is Holy, just and good.' Thirty years after the crucifixion he directs the Ephesians to the keeping the fifth commandment, that they may live long on the *earth* not the land of Canaan. vi: 2, 3. Did not God say that Abraham kept his commandments, statutes, and laws? This embraced the Sabbath for circumcision, and the Sabbath were then the only laws, or statutes, or commandments written. The fourth commandment was given two thousand years before Abraham was born! Is not the stranger and all within their gates included in the covenant to keep the Sabbath? See Exod. xx: 10. And did not God require them to keep THE Sabbath before he made this covenant with them in Horeb? See Exod. xvi: 27-30. Does not Isaiah say that God will bless the *man*, and the *son* of *man*, and the *sons* of the *stranger*, that keep THE Sabbath? These certainly mean the Gentiles. lvi: 2-3, 6-7. Also, in the lviii. ch. 13, 14, the promise is to all that keep the Sabbath. To what people did*the* Sabbath belong at the destruction of Jerusalem, nearly forty years after the crucifixion? Matt. xxiv: 20. The Gentiles certainly were embraced in the covenant by this time! Why was it Paul's manner always to preach on the seventh day Sabbath to Jews and Gentiles?

By what authority do you call the seventh day Sabbath, the Jewish Sabbath? The bible says it is the Sabbath of the *Lord our God*. And Jesus said that he was the 'Lord of the Sabbath day.' He moreover told the Jews that the Sabbath was made for MAN! Where do you draw the distinguishing line, to show which is and which is not MAN between the *natural seed of Abraham* and the Gentiles? "Is he the God of the Jews only? Is he not also of the [Pg 45]Gentiles? Yes, of the Gentiles also!" Then Paul says 'there is no difference,' and that 'there is no respect of persons with God.' Is it not clear, then, that the Sabbath was made for Adam and his posterity, the whole family of *man*? How very fearful you are that God's people should keep the bible Sabbath! You say, 'let us be cautious, lest we disinherit ourselves by seeking the inheritance under the wrong covenant.' Your meaning is, not to seek to keep the Sabbath covenant, but the one made to Abraham. If you can tell us what precept there is in the Abrahamic covenant that we must now keep to be *saved*, that is not embraced in the one given at Mount Sinai, then we will endeavor to keep that too, with the Sabbath of the Lord our God. If the Sabbath, as you say, is abolished, why do you, JOSEPH MARSH, continue to call the first day of the week the Sabbath. See V. T., 15th July. If you profess to utter the VOICE OF TRUTH from the bible, do be consistent, and also willing that *other papers*, besides yours and the Advent Herald, should give the present truth to the flock of God. I say let it go with lightning speed, every way, as does the political news by the electric telegraph. If the whole law and the prophets hang on the commandments, and by keeping them we enter into life, how will you, or I, enter in if we do not 'keep the commandments.' See Exod. xvi: 28-30. Jesus says, "therefore whosoever shall break one of these least commandments and shall teach men so, shall be called the least in the kingdom," &c. "Fear God and keep his commandments, for this is the whole duty of man." Amen!

In the xxxi. ch. of Exod., God says, "Wherefore the children of ISRAEL shall keep the Sabbath, to observe the Sabbath throughout their generations for a *perpetual* covenant; it is a *sign* between me and the children of ISRAEL *forever*." 16, 17 v. *Who are the true Israelites?* Answer, God's people. Hear Paul: "Is he the God of the Jews only? Is he not also of the Gentiles? Yes, of the Gentiles also; from uncircumcision through *faith*." Rom. iii: 29, 30. God gave his re-enacted commandment or covenant to the natural Jew in B. C. 1491. They broke this covenant, as he told Moses they would, for which God partially destroyed and dispersed them; God then brought in a new covenant which continued the sign of the Sabbath, which was confirmed by Jesus and his Apostle about 1525 years from the first. See Heb. viii: 8, 10, 13; Rom. ii: 13. Their breaking the first covenant never could [Pg 46]destroy the commandments of God. Therefore this new, or second covenant, made with the house of ISRAEL, Heb. viii: 10 v. (not the natural Jew only,) is indelibly written upon the heart. Now every child takes the name of his parents. Let us see what the angel Gabriel says to Mary concerning her son: "The Lord God will give him the throne of David *his* Father, and he shall reign over the house of Jacob forever." Luke i: 31, 33.

Now the prophecy: "There shall come a star out of *Jacob* and a sceptre shall rise out of *Israel*." Num. Now 1735 years before Jesus was born, God changed Jacob's name to *Israel*, because he prevailed with him. This then is the family name for all who overcome, or prevail. God gave this name to his spiritual child, namely, *Israel*. Then Jesus will 'reign over the house of *Israel* forever.' This must include all that are saved in the everlasting kingdom. Further, Joseph was the natural son of Jacob or *Israel*. In his prophetic view and dying testimony to his children, he says, Joseph is a fruitful bough, from *thence is the shepherd* the stone of *Israel*. Gen. xlix: 22-34. Then this Shepherd (Jesus) is a descendant, and is of the house of *Israel*. Does he not say that he is the Shepherd of the Sheep,—what, of the Jews only? No, but also of the Gentile, 'for the promise is not through the law (of ceremonies) but thro' the righteousness of *faith*.' Rom. iv: 13. Micah says, 'They shall smite the Judge of *Israel*, that IS to BE the RULER in ISRAEL. v: 1, 2. Now Jesus never was a *Judge* nor *Ruler* in *Israel*. This, then, is a prophecy in the future, that he will judge, and be the Ruler over the whole house of *Israel*. All the family, both natural Jew and Gentile, will assume the family name, the *whole Israel* of God. The angel Gabriel's message, then, is clear; David is the Father of Jesus, according to the flesh, and Jacob, or rather Israel his Father, and Jesus reigns over the house of Israel forever. Paul says, 'He is not a Jew which is one outwardly, but he is a Jew which is one inwardly.' Rom. ii. 'There is no difference between the Jew and the Greek, (or Gentile) for they are not all *Israel* which are of *Israel*, neither because they are the seed of Abraham are they all children.' Why? Because the children of the promise, of Isaac (is the true seed.) ix. and x. ch. To the Gallatinns he says, 'Now to Abraham (the Grandfather of Israel) and his seed were the promises made; not to many, but as of one and to thy seed, which is CHRIST—then says, there is neither Jew nor Greek—but one in Christ Jesus, and if[Pg 47]ye be Christ then are ye Abraham's seed and heirs according to the promise.' iii. 'And as many as walk according to this rule, peace be on them, and mercy, and upon the ISRAEL of God.' vi. This, then, is the name of the whole family in heaven; Christ is God's only Son and lawful heir; none but the true seed can be joint heirs with Christ in the covenant made with Abraham. Ezekiel's prophecy in xxxvii. chapter, God says 'he will bring up out of their *graves* the WHOLE HOUSE OF ISRAEL,' 'and I'll put my spirit in you and ye shall *live*.' 12-14. If God here means any other than the spiritual *Israel*, then Universalism is true—for the *whole* house of natural Israel did not die in faith; if the wicked Jews are to be raised and live before God, then will *all* the wicked! For God is no respecter of persons: 'And the heathen shall know that I the Lord do sanctify *Israel* when my sanctuary shall be in the midst of them forever more.' 28 v. Here, then, we prove, that the dead and living saints are the whole *Israel* of God, and the Covenant and Sign is binding on them into the gates of the holy city. Rev. xx: 14.

[Pg 48]

RECAPITULATION

Page 3. *When was the Sabbath instituted?* Here we have endeavored to show when, and how it continued until its re-enactment on Mount Sinai.

Page 9. *Has the Sabbath been abolished since the seventh day of creation? If so, when, and where is the proof?* Here we believe we have adduced incontestible proof from the scriptures; from the two separate codes of laws given, viz: the first on tables of stone, called by God prophets, Jesus, and his Apostle. 3. The commandments of God. 2d code, the Book of Moses, as written from the mouth of God, the book of ceremonies, combining ecclesiastical and civil law, which Paul shows was nailed to the cross with all *their Sabbaths* as *carnal commandments*, because their feasts commenced and ended with a Sabbath. See Lev. xxiii.

Please read from 16th page onward, how Jesus and the Apostle make the distinction.

Page 27. *Was the seventh day Sabbath ever changed? If so, when, and for what reason?* Here we find, by examining the proofs set forth by those who favor and insist upon the change, that there is not one passage of scripture in the bible to sustain it, but to the contrary, that Jesus kept it and gave directions about it at the destruction of Jerusalem. Paul also, and other Apostles taught how we were to keep the commandments.

Page 42. 4th, The History which is uncontroverted.

5th, The time when the Sabbath commences.

6th, Who are true Israel.

Made in the USA
Columbia, SC
04 October 2023